# ADDRESSES

# 2000

Name

Address

Fax/Email

Phone(s)

Name

Address

Fax/Email

Phone(s)

Name Angelo Sant

Address 64603 Tipperary

Washington MI Fax/Email 48095

Phone(s)

Name Annette + John Parrish

Address 9065 Shortcut Rd,

Ira MI Fax/Email

Phone(s) 716-4132

# Aa

Name   Annie Casha

Address   758 E. Fox Hill Dr,

Bloomfield Hills          Fax/Email   248-339-1286

Phone(s)

Name

Address

Fax/Email

Phone(s)

Name

Address

Fax/Email

Phone(s)

Name

Address

Fax/Email

Phone(s)

# Aa

Name

Address

Fax/Email

Phone(s)

Name

Address

Fax/Email

Phone(s)

Name

Address

Fax/Email

Phone(s)

Name

Address

Fax/Email

Phone(s)

Name  Blue Cross

Address

Fax/Email

Phone(s)  465 - 1988

Name  Betty Dolan

Address  1900 River Rd,

Unit B2  Fax/Email  Marysville 48040

Phone(s)

Name  Bo Richs 17 - Hays

Address

Fax/Email

Phone(s)  263 - 0 450

Name

Address

Fax/Email

Phone(s)

# Bb

Name

Address

Fax/Email

Phone(s)

Name

Address

Fax/Email

Phone(s)

Name

Address

Fax/Email

Phone(s)

Name

Address

Fax/Email

Phone(s)

# Bb

Name

Address

Fax/Email

Phone(s)

Name

Address

Fax/Email

Phone(s)

Name

Address

Fax/Email

Phone(s)

Name

Address

Fax/Email

Phone(s)

Name

Address

Fax/Email

Phone(s)

Name

Address

Fax/Email

Phone(s)

Name

Address

Fax/Email

Phone(s)

Name

Address

Fax/Email

Phone(s)

C

# Cc

Name

Address

Fax/Email

Phone(s)

Name

Address

Fax/Email

Phone(s)

Name

Address

Fax/Email

Phone(s)

Name

Address

Fax/Email

Phone(s)

# Cc

Name

Address

Fax/Email

Phone(s)

Name

Address

Fax/Email

Phone(s)

Name

Address

Fax/Email

Phone(s)

Name

Address

Fax/Email

Phone(s)

Name

Address

Fax/Email

Phone(s)


Name

Address

Fax/Email

Phone(s)


Name

Address

Fax/Email

Phone(s)


Name

Address

Fax/Email

Phone(s)

# Dd

Name

Address

Fax/Email

Phone(s)

Name

Address

Fax/Email

Phone(s)

Name

Address

Fax/Email

Phone(s)

Name

Address

Fax/Email

Phone(s)

# Dd

Name

Address

Fax/Email

Phone(s)

Name

Address

Fax/Email

Phone(s)

Name

Address

Fax/Email

Phone(s)

Name

Address

Fax/Email

Phone(s)

Name

Address

Fax/Email

Phone(s)

Name

Address

Fax/Email

Phone(s)

Name

Address

Fax/Email

Phone(s)

Name

Address

Fax/Email

Phone(s)

E

# Ee

Name

Address

Fax/Email

Phone(s)

Name

Address

Fax/Email

Phone(s)

Name

Address

Fax/Email

Phone(s)

Name

Address

Fax/Email

Phone(s)

# Ee

Name

Address

Fax/Email

Phone(s)

Name

Address

Fax/Email

Phone(s)

Name

Address

Fax/Email

Phone(s)

Name

Address

Fax/Email

Phone(s)

Name

Address

Fax/Email

Phone(s)


Name

Address

Fax/Email

Phone(s)


Name

Address

Fax/Email

Phone(s)


Name

Address

Fax/Email

Phone(s)

F

# Ff

Name

Address

Fax/Email

Phone(s)


Name

Address

Fax/Email

Phone(s)


Name

Address

Fax/Email

Phone(s)


Name

Address

Fax/Email

Phone(s)

# Ff

Name

Address

Fax/Email

Phone(s)


Name

Address

Fax/Email

Phone(s)


Name

Address

Fax/Email

Phone(s)


Name

Address

Fax/Email

Phone(s)

Name
_____

Address
_____

                          Fax/Email
_____

Phone(s)
_____


Name
_____

Address
_____

                          Fax/Email
_____

Phone(s)
_____


Name
_____

Address
_____

                          Fax/Email
_____

Phone(s)
_____


Name
_____

Address
_____

                          Fax/Email
_____

Phone(s)
_____

G

# Gg

Name

Address

Fax/Email

Phone(s)

Name

Address

Fax/Email

Phone(s)

Name

Address

Fax/Email

Phone(s)

Name

Address

Fax/Email

Phone(s)

# Gg

Name

Address

Fax/Email

Phone(s)

Name

Address

Fax/Email

Phone(s)

Name

Address

Fax/Email

Phone(s)

Name

Address

Fax/Email

Phone(s)

Name

Address

Fax/Email

Phone(s)


Name

Address

Fax/Email

Phone(s)


Name

Address

Fax/Email

Phone(s)


Name

Address

Fax/Email

Phone(s)

H

# Hh

Name

Address

Fax/Email

Phone(s)

Name

Address

Fax/Email

Phone(s)

Name

Address

Fax/Email

Phone(s)

Name

Address

Fax/Email

Phone(s)

# Hh

Name

Address

Fax/Email

Phone(s)


Name

Address

Fax/Email

Phone(s)


Name

Address

Fax/Email

Phone(s)


Name

Address

Fax/Email

Phone(s)

Name

Address

Fax/Email

Phone(s)


Name

Address

Fax/Email

Phone(s)


Name

Address

Fax/Email

Phone(s)


Name

Address

Fax/Email

Phone(s)

I

# Ii

Name

Address

Fax/Email

Phone(s)

Name

Address

Fax/Email

Phone(s)

Name

Address

Fax/Email

Phone(s)

Name

Address

Fax/Email

Phone(s)

# Ii

Name

Address

Fax/Email

Phone(s)

Name

Address

Fax/Email

Phone(s)

Name

Address

Fax/Email

Phone(s)

Name

Address

Fax/Email

Phone(s)

Name

Address

Fax/Email

Phone(s)


Name

Address

Fax/Email

Phone(s)


Name

Address

Fax/Email

Phone(s)


Name

Address

Fax/Email

Phone(s)

# Jj

Name

Address

Fax/Email

Phone(s)

Name

Address

Fax/Email

Phone(s)

Name

Address

Fax/Email

Phone(s)

Name

Address

Fax/Email

Phone(s)

# Jj

Name

Address

Fax/Email

Phone(s)

Name

Address

Fax/Email

Phone(s)

Name

Address

Fax/Email

Phone(s)

Name

Address

Fax/Email

Phone(s)

Name

Address

Fax/Email

Phone(s)


Name

Address

Fax/Email

Phone(s)


Name

Address

Fax/Email

Phone(s)


Name

Address

Fax/Email

Phone(s)

K

# Kk

Name

Address

Fax/Email

Phone(s)

Name

Address

Fax/Email

Phone(s)

Name

Address

Fax/Email

Phone(s)

Name

Address

Fax/Email

Phone(s)

# Kk

Name

Address

Fax/Email

Phone(s)


Name

Address

Fax/Email

Phone(s)


Name

Address

Fax/Email

Phone(s)


Name

Address

Fax/Email

Phone(s)

Name

Address

Fax/Email

Phone(s)

Name

Address

Fax/Email

Phone(s)

Name

Address

Fax/Email

Phone(s)

Name

Address

Fax/Email

Phone(s)

L

# Ll

Name

Address

Fax/Email

Phone(s)


Name

Address

Fax/Email

Phone(s)


Name

Address

Fax/Email

Phone(s)


Name

Address

Fax/Email

Phone(s)

# Ll

Name

Address

Fax/Email

Phone(s)

Name

Address

Fax/Email

Phone(s)

Name

Address

Fax/Email

Phone(s)

Name

Address

Fax/Email

Phone(s)

Name

Address

Fax/Email

Phone(s)


Name

Address

Fax/Email

Phone(s)


Name

Address

Fax/Email

Phone(s)


Name

Address

Fax/Email

Phone(s)

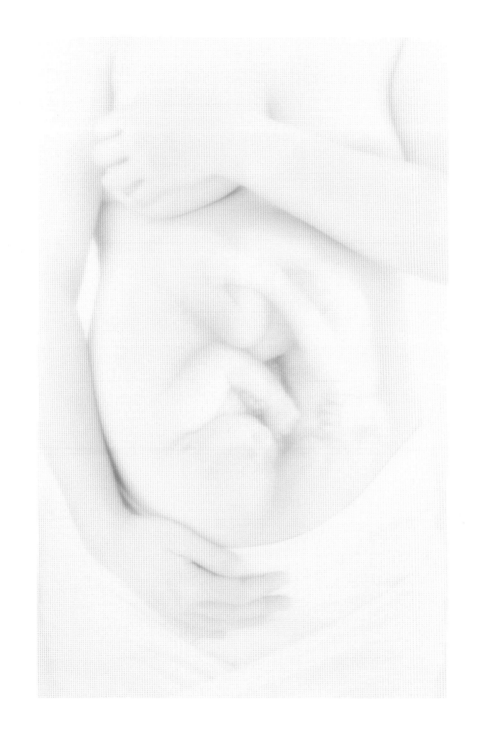

# Mm

Name

Address

Fax/Email

Phone(s)

Name

Address

Fax/Email

Phone(s)

Name

Address

Fax/Email

Phone(s)

Name

Address

Fax/Email

Phone(s)

# Mm

Name

Address

Fax/Email

Phone(s)

Name

Address

Fax/Email

Phone(s)

Name

Address

Fax/Email

Phone(s)

Name

Address

Fax/Email

Phone(s)

Name

Address

Fax/Email

Phone(s)


Name

Address

Fax/Email

Phone(s)


Name

Address

Fax/Email

Phone(s)


Name

Address

Fax/Email

Phone(s)

# Nn

Name

Address

Fax/Email

Phone(s)

Name

Address

Fax/Email

Phone(s)

Name

Address

Fax/Email

Phone(s)

Name

Address

Fax/Email

Phone(s)

# Nn

Name

Address

Fax/Email

Phone(s)

Name

Address

Fax/Email

Phone(s)

Name

Address

Fax/Email

Phone(s)

Name

Address

Fax/Email

Phone(s)

Name

Address

Fax/Email

Phone(s)

Name

Address

Fax/Email

Phone(s)

Name

Address

Fax/Email

Phone(s)

Name

Address

Fax/Email

Phone(s)

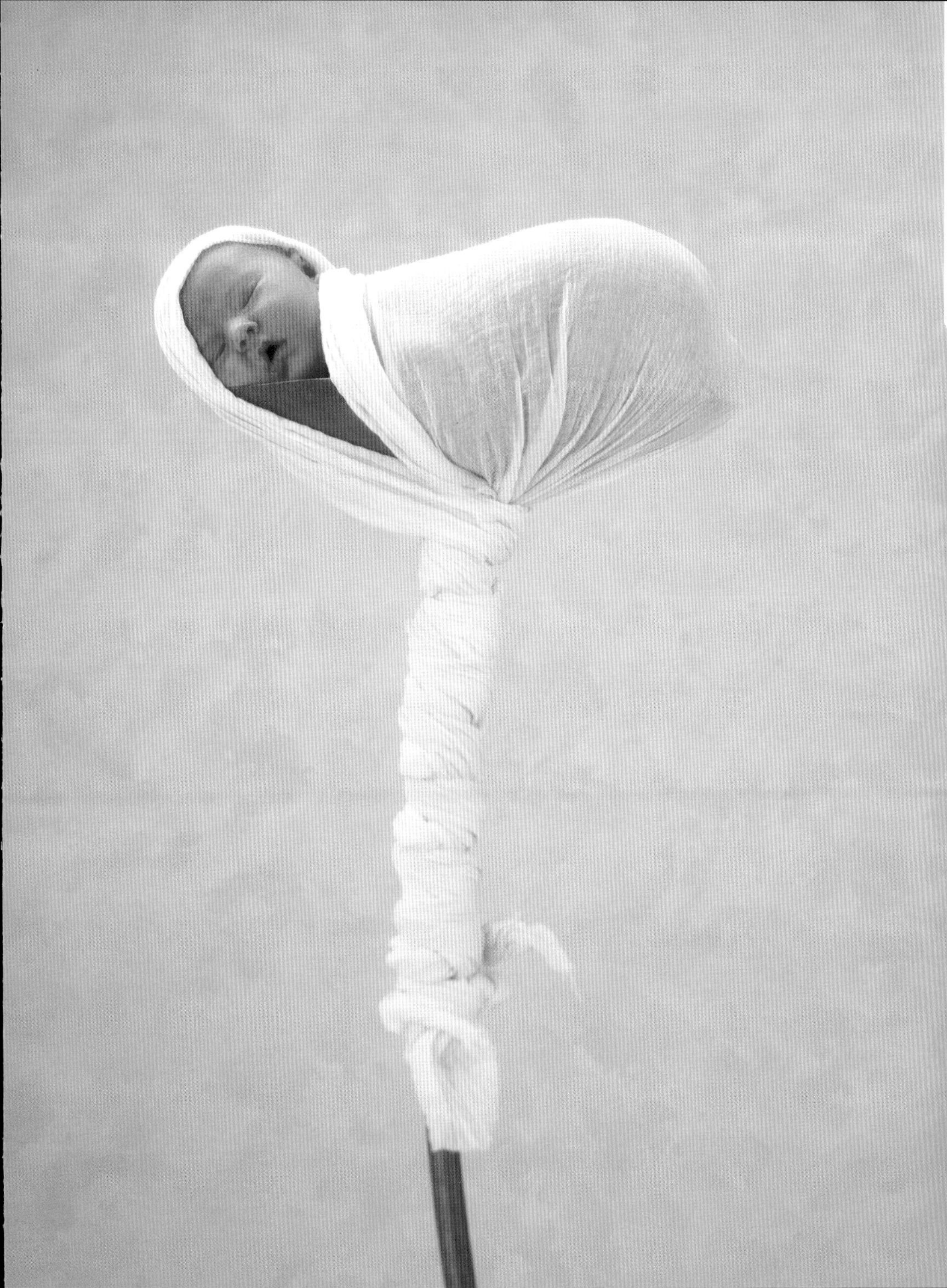

0

# Oo

Name

Address

Fax/Email

Phone(s)

Name

Address

Fax/Email

Phone(s)

Name

Address

Fax/Email

Phone(s)

Name

Address

Fax/Email

Phone(s)

# Oo

Name

Address

Fax/Email

Phone(s)


Name

Address

Fax/Email

Phone(s)


Name

Address

Fax/Email

Phone(s)


Name

Address

Fax/Email

Phone(s)

Name

Address

Fax/Email

Phone(s)


Name

Address

Fax/Email

Phone(s)


Name

Address

Fax/Email

Phone(s)


Name

Address

Fax/Email

Phone(s)

P

# Pp

Name

Address

Fax/Email

Phone(s)

Name

Address

Fax/Email

Phone(s)

Name

Address

Fax/Email

Phone(s)

Name

Address

Fax/Email

Phone(s)

# Pp

Name

Address

Fax/Email

Phone(s)

Name

Address

Fax/Email

Phone(s)

Name

Address

Fax/Email

Phone(s)

Name

Address

Fax/Email

Phone(s)

# Qq

Name

Address

Fax/Email

Phone(s)

Name

Address

Fax/Email

Phone(s)

Name

Address

Fax/Email

Phone(s)

Name

Address

Fax/Email

Phone(s)

# Qq

Name

Address

Fax/Email

Phone(s)

Name

Address

Fax/Email

Phone(s)

Name

Address

Fax/Email

Phone(s)

Name

Address

Fax/Email

Phone(s)

Q

Name

Address

Fax/Email

Phone(s)


Name

Address

Fax/Email

Phone(s)


Name

Address

Fax/Email

Phone(s)


Name

Address

Fax/Email

Phone(s)

# Rr

Name

Address

Fax/Email

Phone(s)

Name

Address

Fax/Email

Phone(s)

Name

Address

Fax/Email

Phone(s)

Name

Address

Fax/Email

Phone(s)

# Rr

Name

Address

Fax/Email

Phone(s)

Name

Address

Fax/Email

Phone(s)

Name

Address

Fax/Email

Phone(s)

Name

Address

Fax/Email

Phone(s)

Name

Address

Fax/Email

Phone(s)


Name

Address

Fax/Email

Phone(s)


Name

Address

Fax/Email

Phone(s)


Name

Address

Fax/Email

Phone(s)

S

# Ss

Name

Address

Fax/Email

Phone(s)

Name

Address

Fax/Email

Phone(s)

Name

Address

Fax/Email

Phone(s)

Name

Address

Fax/Email

Phone(s)

# Ss

Name

Address

Fax/Email

Phone(s)

Name

Address

Fax/Email

Phone(s)

Name

Address

Fax/Email

Phone(s)

Name

Address

Fax/Email

Phone(s)

Name

Address

Fax/Email

Phone(s)

Name

Address

Fax/Email

Phone(s)

Name

Address

Fax/Email

Phone(s)

Name

Address

Fax/Email

Phone(s)

# Tt

Name

Address

Fax/Email

Phone(s)

Name

Address

Fax/Email

Phone(s)

Name

Address

Fax/Email

Phone(s)

Name

Address

Fax/Email

Phone(s)

# Tt

Name

Address

Fax/Email

Phone(s)

Name

Address

Fax/Email

Phone(s)

Name

Address

Fax/Email

Phone(s)

Name

Address

Fax/Email

Phone(s)

Name

Address

Fax/Email

Phone(s)

Name

Address

Fax/Email

Phone(s)

Name

Address

Fax/Email

Phone(s)

Name

Address

Fax/Email

Phone(s)

U

# Uu

Name

Address

Fax/Email

Phone(s)

Name

Address

Fax/Email

Phone(s)

Name

Address

Fax/Email

Phone(s)

Name

Address

Fax/Email

Phone(s)

# Uu

Name

Address

Fax/Email

Phone(s)


Name

Address

Fax/Email

Phone(s)


Name

Address

Fax/Email

Phone(s)


Name

Address

Fax/Email

Phone(s)

Name

Address

Fax/Email

Phone(s)


Name

Address

Fax/Email

Phone(s)


Name

Address

Fax/Email

Phone(s)


Name

Address

Fax/Email

Phone(s)

V

# Vv

Name

Address

Fax/Email

Phone(s)

Name

Address

Fax/Email

Phone(s)

Name

Address

Fax/Email

Phone(s)

Name

Address

Fax/Email

Phone(s)

# Vv

Name

Address

Fax/Email

Phone(s)

Name

Address

Fax/Email

Phone(s)

Name

Address

Fax/Email

Phone(s)

Name

Address

Fax/Email

Phone(s)

Name

Address

Fax/Email

Phone(s)


Name

Address

Fax/Email

Phone(s)


Name

Address

Fax/Email

Phone(s)


Name

Address

Fax/Email

Phone(s)

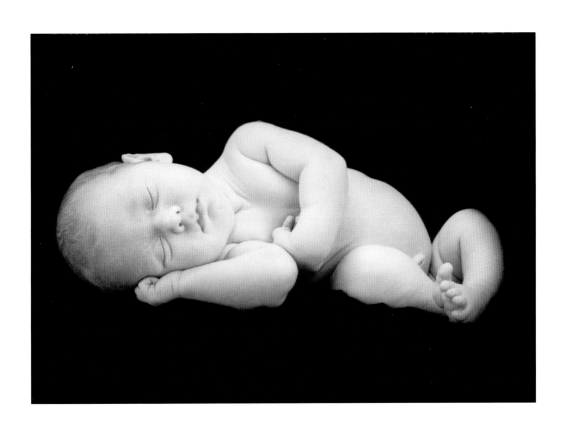

W

# Ww

Name

Address

Fax/Email

Phone(s)

Name

Address

Fax/Email

Phone(s)

Name

Address

Fax/Email

Phone(s)

Name

Address

Fax/Email

Phone(s)

# Ww

Name

Address

Fax/Email

Phone(s)

Name

Address

Fax/Email

Phone(s)

Name

Address

Fax/Email

Phone(s)

Name

Address

Fax/Email

Phone(s)

Name

Address

Fax/Email

Phone(s)

Name

Address

Fax/Email

Phone(s)

Name

Address

Fax/Email

Phone(s)

Name

Address

Fax/Email

Phone(s)

X
Y
Z

# XYZ

Name

Address

Fax/Email

Phone(s)


Name

Address

Fax/Email

Phone(s)


Name

Address

Fax/Email

Phone(s)


Name

Address

Fax/Email

Phone(s)

# XYZ

Name

Address

Fax/Email

Phone(s)

Name

Address

Fax/Email

Phone(s)

Name

Address

Fax/Email

Phone(s)

Name

Address

Fax/Email

Phone(s)

ANNE GEDDES ™

ISBN-0-7683-2121-2

© Anne Geddes 1999

www.annegeddes.com

Published in 1999 by Photogenique Publishers
(a division of Hodder Moa Beckett)
Studio 3.16, Axis Building, 1 Cleveland Road, Parnell
Auckland, New Zealand

First USA edition published in 1999
by Cedco Publishing Company
100 Pelican Way, San Rafael, CA 94901

Produced by Kel Geddes
Color separations by Image Centre
Printed by Midas Printing Limited, Hong Kong

Please write to us for a FREE FULL COLOR catalog of our
fine Anne Geddes calendars and books, Cedco Publishing Company,
100 Pelican Way, San Rafael, CA 94901
or visit our website: www.cedco.com
10 9 8 7 6 5 4 3 2